The Library of Sexual Health™

THE ENDOCRINE SYSTEM:
Hormones, Growth, and Development

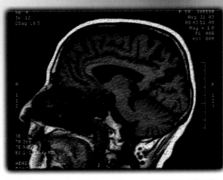

MICHAEL R. WILSON

ROSEN
PUBLISHING®

New York

Published in 2009 by The Rosen Publishing Group, Inc.
29 East 21st Street, New York, NY 10010

Copyright © 2009 by The Rosen Publishing Group, Inc.

First Edition

Library of Congress Cataloging-in-Publication Data

Wilson, Michael R., 1967–
The endocrine system: hormones, growth, and development / Michael R. Wilson.
     p. cm.—(The library of sexual health)
Includes bibliographical references and index.
ISBN-13: 978-1-4358-5062-0 (library binding)
1. Endocrine glands—Juvenile literature. I. Title.
QP187.W557 2009
612.4—dc22

                                                    2008016585

Manufactured in Malaysia

CONTENTS

This book is about the human endocrine system. The endocrine system is made up of a group of organs and the hormones they produce. One way or another, the endocrine system helps to control almost everything about us. More specifically, this book tackles the way the endocrine system influences sexual development, sexual function, and reproduction. It also reveals what happens when things go wrong—the endocrine disorders that, if left untreated, may harm one's sexual health.

The endocrine system is not an easy subject, especially when it comes to how it relates to sexual health. Still, by the time you're through with this book, you should have a good idea of how hormones work. In addition, you'll learn which hormones are most important to sexual development and reproduction, as well as which diseases and conditions are often caused by endocrine disorders.

You'll also find information on the prevention, diagnosis, and treatment of endocrine disorders. What are the signs and symptoms of certain endocrine problems? How do doctors treat those problems? What can people with endocrine disorders do to live healthier and happier lives? You'll find some answers in this book.

How you use the information in this book is up to you. You may find it's useful as a research aid for school reports. Or, maybe you'd like information for use in your own life, or for ideas on how you can help a friend with an endocrine problem. Endocrine system disorders are relatively rare, but they do occur, even among otherwise healthy teenagers. Whatever the case, when you finish reading, check out the Web sites, organizations, and other references that are listed at the end of this book. They're intended to help you learn more about all things related to the endocrine system and sexual health.

If this book sparks your interest in the endocrine system, then use it as a launching point for further investigation. When it comes to endocrinology—the study of the endocrine system—there's a world of information out there waiting to be discovered.

CHAPTER ONE

Endocrine Biology

Body hair. Growth spurts. Puberty. Acne. They're all a part of teenage life, and they're all due to hormones. Our bodies run on hormones. Hormones help control just about everything about us—our blood pressure, how we digest food and process nutrients, our sexual development, reproduction, you name it. Without hormones, our bodies just wouldn't work.

Hormones are tiny molecules that act like mail in the body's chemical messaging system. Changes in the body stimulate the endocrine organs to release specific hormones into the bloodstream. Each endocrine organ sends out millions of hormone molecules at once. Once in the blood, these hormones circulate throughout the body. Before long, they reach almost every cell. Specific types of hormones are destined for specific kinds of cells, called target cells. To be even more precise, specific hormones are destined for specific mailbox-like receptors on those cells. When a hormone, traveling along in the bloodstream, arrives at its target cell and finds its unique receptor, it exits the current and latches on. When a hormone links, or binds, to its receptor, it sets in motion a series of reactions that helps your body to function properly. (The binding involves a chemical process better discussed in chemistry!)

The hormone causes the cell to do something—increase its sodium or potassium concentration, for example, or decrease its calcium levels or begin production of a certain protein. That cellular change, in turn, leads to

The hormones of your endocrine system become more active as you enter your teen years. Hormones are the chemical messengers that direct everything from blood flow to reproduction.

something else, which leads to something else, and on and on. Before you know it, your voice is changing, you're growing taller, and there's a huge pimple in the middle of your forehead. Of course, in the real world, the endocrine system is much more complicated.

ORGANS OF THE ENDOCRINE SYSTEM

The endocrine system is made up of the endocrine organs, the hormones those organs secrete (release), and the reactions these hormones produce. Like all systems, the endocrine system includes a variety of interacting parts.

Endocrine organs are located in many parts of the body, from the brain to the testes (in men) and ovaries (in women). They include the hypothalamus, which is found deep in the middle of the brain; the pituitary gland, which is just below the hypothalamus; and the pineal gland, also in the middle of the brain. In addition, endocrine organs include the thyroid and parathyroid glands, which are located below the jaw; the adrenal glands, which are just above the kidneys; and the thymus gland, which is found in the chest, above the heart. These organs are referred to as glands. Unlike other body organs, glands produce and secrete substances (in this case, hormones) for distribution to the rest of the body.

What does each of these organs do? Let's run through the list, beginning with what you might call the "master" endocrine organ: the hypothalamus. This gland is like an

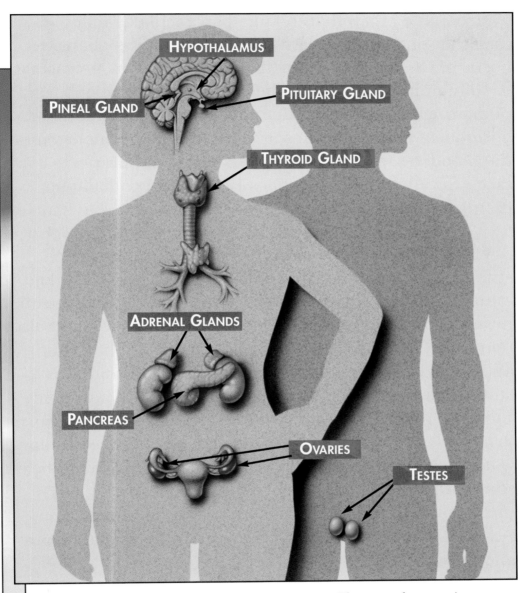

Shown here are the organs of the endocrine system. These are the same in men and women, except for those organs that produce sex hormones. In men, the testes release testosterone. In women, the ovaries release estrogen and progesterone.

overseer, the organ that in large part regulates many of the other endocrine organs. Depending on the changing needs of the body, the hypothalamus produces "releasing" or "inhibiting" hormones. These travel to the neighboring pituitary gland. If the pituitary gland receives "releasing" hormones, then it secretes its own specific hormones into the bloodstream. On the other hand, if the pituitary receives "inhibiting" hormones from the hypothalamus, then it will stop secreting certain hormones.

The pituitary gland produces many hormones, one of which is called growth hormone. Growth hormone stimulates cells throughout the body to grow, divide, and multiply. As a result, bones grow longer and thicker, while muscles grow bigger and stronger. The pituitary gland also releases a hormone called thyroid-stimulating hormone, or TSH, which does exactly what its name implies. It stimulates the thyroid gland to release thyroid hormones, called T3 and T4, which are necessary for the body to turn food into energy. Other hormones released by the pituitary gland include adrenocorticotropic hormone (ACTH), follicle-stimulating hormone (FSH), luteinizing hormone (LH), prolactin, oxytocin, and antidiuretic hormone (ADH). Several of these hormones are important to sexual health and development.

A normally functioning pineal gland is important to sexual development. It works together with the hypothalamus to secrete melatonin. This hormone plays an important role in regulating the body's rhythms, including the reproductive cycle.

The parathyroid glands, found next to the larger thyroid, secrete parathyroid hormone (PTH), which controls calcium concentration in the blood. The adrenal glands, for their part, release steroid hormones including aldosterone, cortisol, and small amounts of testosterone. They also release the "emergency mode" hormones epinephrine and norepinephrine. These are the hormones that kick in to increase your heart rate and blood pressure when you're frightened.

Finally, there is the thymus. The thymus makes thymopoietins and thymosins, which are hormones important to the immune system. The thymus is also the factory for the development of lymphocytes, a type of white blood cell.

There are other endocrine organs as well. The pancreas, for example, produces the hormones insulin and glucagon, which together work to regulate sugar concentration in the blood. The gonads—ovaries in women and testes in men—release the sex hormones. Women's ovaries produce the primary female sex hormones estrogen and progesterone. Estrogen is key to the development of the female reproductive system. Both progesterone and estrogen are important to breast development, the menstrual cycle, and fertility. The testes, on the other hand, produce the primary male sex hormone testosterone (in much larger quantities than the adrenal glands). Testosterone is important in male reproductive organ development and function. While a boy fetus is maturing in the womb, testosterone is critical to early genital development, as well as general growth. During puberty, testosterone causes the testes and penis to increase in size, facial and pubic hair to develop, and the voice to deepen. For adult males, testosterone helps produce sperm and is responsible for the sex drive (libido). Interestingly, the ovaries also normally produce small amounts of testosterone, while the testes produce some estrogen.

Several other body organs and cells that are not normally considered part of the endocrine system also produce hormones that may affect the endocrine system.

HORMONE CONTROLS

Hormone release doesn't just happen on a whim. Instead, it is a highly organized process, with hormone production by one gland dependent on that by others. Think of the endocrine system as a constantly evolving signaling pathway. Something in the body must first send a signal to a hormone-releasing gland to do its work. When that signal is received, the gland will release the right amount of the appropriate hormone. Signals are also sent for glands to stop releasing hormones. Once a hormone triggers the desired response, that response will cause hormone production to decrease. This is called negative feedback. When the levels of certain nutrients in the blood fall outside of a certain range, endocrine glands respond by releasing hormones to correct those levels.

Other hormones are released as a result of a signal from the nervous system, rather than other endocrine organs. For example, epinephrine is released from the adrenal glands in response to stress on the nervous system. Most of the time, however, endocrine glands release their hormones in response to hormonal signals from other endocrine organs.

The main thing to remember about hormone production and control is that it is a complicated, highly interdependent process. Everything depends on everything else, and everything occurs in reaction to the constantly changing environment within the body. The endocrine system is a difficult subject to master, but if you know a little bit about it, you'll find it far easier to understand what happens when things go wrong.

Myths and Facts

MYTH: When a man has trouble becoming sexually aroused—getting an erection, for example—there must be something seriously wrong.

FACT: There could be a hormone problem, but more likely it's due to other factors—lack of interest, distraction, or fatigue, to name a few. The truth is it's normal to not always be interested in sex, as sexual interest and arousal come and go. For most people, there are certainly times when sexual arousal is easy, but it is normal to have times when it is not so easy.

MYTH: Because of hormones, menstruating girls and women are moody.

FACT: Different women have different experiences when it comes to their periods, or menstruation. Some experience wild mood swings, while others hardly notice any major mood changes. It's wrong to assume that a woman's period, when it comes, will be burdensome.

MYTH: The best way to treat hormone problems is through hormone therapy—taking artificial hormones to bring the endocrine system back into balance.

FACT: In some cases, hormone therapy may help. However, effective treatment typically involves much more, including changes in diet and lifestyle. Hormone issues can result from a variety of factors, including chemicals in the environment, poor nutrition, and a body's natural cycles. As these all affect the body differently, hormone problems should be tackled from all angles. Some people benefit from counseling or support groups. Others are helped by therapeutic drugs. When it comes to the endocrine system, everyone is different.

CHAPTER TWO

Endocrine Conditions and Diseases

I n a perfectly functioning body, the endocrine system does its job completely under the radar. You never even know it is there. Sometimes, however, things do go wrong. Unfortunately, these things could fill an entire book—and a college-level textbook at that. For our purposes, we can narrow these down. We'll just focus on the endocrine issues associated with sexual health.

WHEN THINGS GO WRONG

Problems with the endocrine system arise when things don't work as they should. For instance, too much of a hormone might be released by one gland or too little by another. In some cases, there might not be enough functioning receptors on cells to take up the hormones already circulating in the blood. In other cases, the body's waste-removal and filtration organs—the liver and kidneys—don't do their job. As a result, hormone concentration levels in the blood can build to dangerous levels. Other factors influencing the endocrine system include old age, illness, genetics, and environmental pollutants. Some people are born with endocrine disorders. Others develop problems resulting from injuries, surgical mistakes, or illnesses. There are many ways that the endocrine system can be compromised, or harmed.

In many cases, endocrine issues affect sexual health, creating problems with sexual development, infertility, and birth defects, among other things. Some endocrine issues are caused by the presence of synthetic chemicals such as dioxins and PCBs in the water, food, or air. In the body, these chemicals can mimic natural hormones, leading the endocrine system to operate as though it has adequate levels of certain hormones when, in fact, it does not.

The endocrine system is by no means to blame for all sexual health issues. Various other environmental, social, and physical factors also play a role, sometimes all at once. Occasionally, however, a physician may suspect that a patient's poor sexual health is being caused by a specific hormonal problem. When this is the case, a specialist called an endocrinologist may be brought in to diagnose and treat an endocrine disorder. Endocrinologists also treat hormonal "problems" such as menopause, which really aren't problems at all but are just a natural part of the human life cycle.

MENOPAUSE

Menopause is that time in life, usually around the age of fifty, when a woman stops producing eggs and having her period. The first thing to realize about menopause is that it is normal. Every woman who lives long enough goes through it eventually. Some experience it early, some late. But one day, it happens.

When menopause does occur, a woman cannot become pregnant using natural methods. Her ovaries no longer produce eggs, so fertilization (which requires an egg and the male's sperm) cannot occur. Menopause doesn't happen overnight. It is a process that takes place over time, often over the course of several years.

As menopause progresses, the ovaries stop producing eggs and also produce less and less of the sex hormones estrogen and progesterone. "Less and less" can be mis-leading, however, because it's not a steady decline. Instead, it's more of a roller-coaster ride, with hormone levels high one day, back to "normal" the next, high again the following day, and then low a day after that. Over time they go down, but day-to-day, for some women anyway, hormone levels can fluctuate and it can often seem like they're out of control.

What happens then? Sometimes, a woman going through menopause will get her period. Sometimes, she won't. Those pulsating hormones may cause her to experience hot flashes and mood swings and, in some cases, depression. She might lose interest in sex, or be interested one day but repulsed the next. She might also experience physical changes—vaginal dryness, for example—that make sex uncomfortable or unappealing.

There is a variety of ways to help women deal with menopause. One treatment is known as hormone therapy, or hormone replacement therapy (HRT). This involves taking medically prescribed synthetic estrogen and progestin (progesterone). The drugs reduce hot flashes, treat vaginal dryness, and decrease the rate of bone loss (osteoporosis). The replacement hormones in the drugs

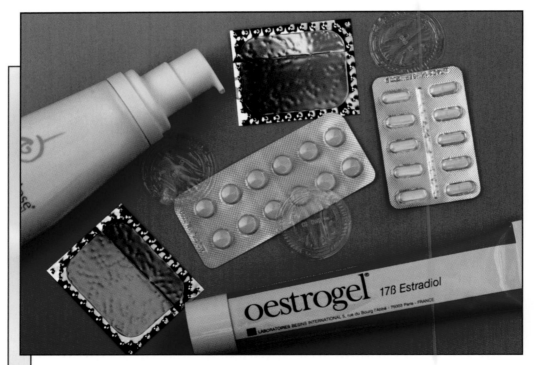

Many women use hormone replacement therapy (HRT) to help them cope with menopause. Devices used to deliver replacement hormones include gels, patches, tablets, and gelatin capsules.

serve to smooth out the ups and downs of menopause. This helps to reduce the symptoms and generally make life easier during a time that, for many women, is exceedingly difficult. Of course, many women don't receive any treatment at all for menopause. Others start treatment and then decide they no longer need it. Treatment, including hormone dosage, depends on the individual.

Menopausal women may find comfort in talking to a support group. This is a group that meets regularly to talk about their experiences with menopause and discuss ways to cope. Some women find that professional counseling helps them to get through menopause. Others find it helpful to take natural or alternative approaches to dealing with menopause. For example, they might take supplements to improve bone health, or maintain a special diet rich in nutritious fruits and vegetables. Getting lots of exercise also helps. Physical activity not only distracts a woman's body and mind from the trials of menopause, but it also helps maintain healthy bones and a healthy heart.

ENDOCRINE DISORDERS AND SEXUAL HEALTH

Precocious puberty. Breast cancer. Erectile dysfunction. Infertility. Low testosterone. Menstrual cycle disorders. Premenstrual syndrome. You have certainly heard of some of these. Maybe you have even experienced one or two—or at least know someone who has. There are all kinds of disorders related to reproduction, sex, sexuality, and sexual health in general. We'll cover some of them here before moving on to discuss ways to cope with them.

Menstrual Cycle Disorders

Menopause is perfectly normal among middle-aged women. However, there are two hormone-related menstrual cycle conditions that sometimes occur in younger women and are not normal: oligomenorrhea and amenorrhea. Oligomenorrhea occurs when a woman has her period, but it comes less frequently or regularly than it should. Amenorrhea, on the other hand, is the abnormal absence of menstrual periods.

Primary amenorrhea is diagnosed in girls who go through puberty but still haven't had their first period by the age of sixteen. Secondary amenorrhea is diagnosed when women with previously established periods stop menstruating for more than three to six months. Both primary and secondary amenorrhea can be caused by an eating disorder. Amenorrhea is also diagnosed in over-trained athletes with extremely low body fat. Girls who are excessively underweight don't take in enough calories for their bodies to function normally. Without adequate food, their body systems, including certain endocrine functions, shut down. Menstrual bleeding then stops because the body must conserve resources for more critical functions such as maintaining the cardiovascular system.

Problems with the hypothalamus, pituitary gland, or ovaries usually cause menstrual cycle disorders. For instance, if the hypothalamus can't release adequate gonadotropin releasing hormone (GnRH), then there may not be enough follicle-stimulating hormone (FSH) or luteinizing hormone (LH) for menstruation to occur.

A young woman having menstruation problems should go to her physician for a complete physical exam, including a pelvic exam. Her physician will take her medical history to determine if there may be an underlying cause for the condition. The exam will include a thorough analysis of the woman's sexual development, testing of

Excessive training for athletic activities such as gymnastics, ballet, and long-distance running can cause endocrine system problems in young women.

hormone levels, and possibly testing for diseases such as diabetes. If the woman is sexually active, then a pregnancy test can rule out pregnancy as the reason for the absence of periods. If there is reason to believe that the hypothalamus or pituitary gland is not functioning correctly, then brain magnetic resonance imaging (MRI) technology may be used to obtain images to help determine if the gland is normal.

Treatment of amenorrhea or oligomenorrhea depends on test results and may include surgery (to remove an ovarian tumor, for example) or hormone therapy to correct hormone imbalances.

Polycystic Ovary Syndrome

Polycystic ovary syndrome, or PCOS, is a condition in which a woman develops multiple cysts on her ovaries. Ovarian cysts are small, sac-like growths that are common and generally harmless. However, PCOS is a serious issue that can lead to menstrual cycle irregularities, infertility, and hormone problems. It can also cause cardiovascular (heart) issues and an increased risk of uterine cancer. Women with PCOS typically have higher levels of androgens, or male hormones. As a result, these women may have increased hair growth on their face, chest, stomach, back, hands, and feet. When a woman with PCOS gets pregnant, she has a higher risk of miscarriage, gestational (baby-related) diabetes, and premature delivery.

PCOS and the Menstrual Cycle

Women with polycystic ovary syndrome (PCOS) usually have trouble with their menstrual cycles due to malfunctioning ovaries.

In normal ovary

Each month, about 20 follicles start to grow; usually only one matures

At ovulation, mature egg released from follicle, moves into fallopian tube

Mature follicle releases progesterone; uterine lining thickens, period follows

Fallopian tube

Uterus

Follicle
Sac full of fluid surrounding egg

Ovary

In PCOS ovary

Body doesn't make hormones for an egg to mature

Follicles grow, but none mature; some remain as cysts

Cyst

• No egg released, no progesterone produced; uterine lining doesn't thicken

Ovary

PCOS occurs in nearly 10 percent of women of childbearing age. More than five million American women have PCOS, but their symptoms often go unnoticed, so many don't even realize that they are affected. Many others go undiagnosed because they think their symptoms are due to some other condition.

What causes PCOS? That's up for debate. Most scientists think genes are involved—that is, it's hereditary and can be passed from one generation to the next. It's also agreed that hormones play a role. Many women with PCOS have too much insulin (produced in the pancreas), which in turn causes the ovaries and adrenal glands to produce too much of the male sex hormones, androgens. The ovarian cysts in PCOS are also a result of hormone imbalances—in this case, too little of the female hormones estrogen and progesterone.

There is no cure for PCOS. Symptoms can be treated, however, with anything from improved diet, weight loss, and regular exercise to prescription medication. Some women take birth control pills as part of their treatment. The pills lower androgen levels and help regulate the menstrual cycle. Other women take diabetes medications to help with insulin levels and uptake, as well as to lower their testosterone production. Women with PCOS who want to become pregnant may succeed by taking fertility medications to stimulate ovulation. Some women take medications called "anti-androgens" in order to reduce the male characteristics (excess body hair, for example) that are brought about by PCOS.

Whatever the case, when a woman with PCOS goes for medical evaluation, her doctor will certainly begin with a physical exam and then follow it up by testing for hormone levels in the bloodstream. The doctor may also order an ultrasound scan, or sonogram, to obtain an image of the ovaries. Treatment depends on the individual's needs and on what the doctor finds.

There is a national support group for those with PCOS, the Polycystic Ovarian Syndrome Association, Inc. You can visit its site, www.pcosupport.org.

Erectile Dysfunction

Erectile dysfunction is also known as impotence. It is a man's inability to get an erection, and it occurs when there is reduced blood flow to the penis. Erectile dysfunction can be a serious problem because it makes having sexual intercourse difficult or even impossible. That, in turn, can complicate sexual relationships and make it impossible to have children without some sort of assistance (artificial insemination, for example). Erectile dysfunction can also be embarrassing. An estimated thirty million American men have erectile dysfunction.

There are several reasons why men have erection troubles. Among them are emotional problems brought on by stress, drug or alcohol abuse, smoking, and the side effects of prescription medication. Physical problems can also cause erectile dysfunction. A serious injury to the groin, for example, may make it impossible to get or maintain an erection.

And, of course, there are hormones. For some men, their erection problems can be blamed on low levels of testosterone. An estimated five million American men have low testosterone. In many cases, low testosterone levels result naturally from aging. This is part of the reason why more elderly men have erectile dysfunction than their younger counterparts. Low testosterone can also result from an injury to the testes, chemotherapy or radiation treatment, or genetic problems. Some men can blame erectile dysfunction on their pituitary glands. If the pituitary is not functioning correctly, then it can't stimulate the testes to produce the right levels of testosterone. Other men may have a problem higher up the endocrine signal pathway, in the hypothalamus, the organ that controls the pituitary.

Some drugs cause the testes to lower testosterone production. Anabolic steroids, for example, cause the pituitary gland to stop signaling the testes to produce testosterone.

Low testosterone is an endocrine problem in and of itself, with erectile dysfunction being just one of several possible symptoms. A man with low testosterone may experience decreased libido (sex drive) and/or a lowered sperm count, which could result in infertility. Insufficient amounts of testosterone may also cause the development of feminine-looking breasts (a condition called gynecomastia), decreased muscle mass, and depression.

The symptoms discussed here may be caused by lowered testosterone, but the only way to know for sure is through blood tests. In most cases, the blood is tested not only for testosterone but also for the hormones LH, FSH, and prolactin. If the doctor can get a good idea of the balance of hormones in the blood, then he or she will know how to go about treatment. If it does turn out to be a problem with low testosterone, then treatment may include testosterone replacement therapy. Synthetic testosterone may be administered through injection, pills, skin patches, or gels. If the doctor finds the patient has a disease that is causing the low testosterone levels, then he or she will probably discuss ways to treat that

Heavily muscled bodybuilders are known to use anabolic steroids, which can cause unnatural imbalances in hormone levels.

particular disease. For instance, a problem with testosterone levels may be caused by a tumor in the pituitary gland. Only imaging technology such as a CT scan or MRI could show this for certain. Treatment of the tumor may require medication, surgery, radiation therapy, and/or chemotherapy.

Congenital Adrenal Hyperplasia and Intersex Disorders

Congenital adrenal hyperplasia (CAH) is an inherited set of genetic disorders of the adrenal glands. In CAH, these glands do not properly produce corticosteroid hormones, which include cortisol and aldosterone. The condition, which is usually diagnosed in early childhood, occurs in both males and females.

People with CAH have troubles with their energy levels, blood-sugar levels, and blood pressure. They're particularly prone to bad reactions in situations that involve physical stress—as when one is injured, or even during exercise. Normal growth and development may also be compromised in those with CAH.

In many cases, people with CAH have too much androgen production. Excessive androgens are produced to make up for inadequate cortisol production. This results in rapid early growth and often causes a premature onset of puberty, with the development of secondary sex characteristics such as pubic hair coming in early childhood. Girls with CAH may develop masculine features, including facial hair. They may also be born with male-like external genitals in addition to their normal internal female genitals. When this happens, their condition is called an intersex disorder. Women with CAH often experience problems with their periods and even infertility.

CAH can be dangerous, but it can also be embarrassing. For children with CAH, many of the issues are related to fitting in socially. Later, in adulthood, the main concern might shift more toward issues of fertility.

CAH is a genetic disorder. For this reason, CAH can often be detected before birth through prenatal genetic testing. After birth, routine newborn screening can reveal CAH. As is the case with most hormone problems, CAH can be treated using hormone therapy. The idea is to raise corticosteroids to normal levels. Depending on the individual, this may involve taking cortisol, aldosterone, or both. A good resource and support group for those with CAH can be found online at www.congentialadrenalhyperplasia.org.

Infertility

Infertility is the inability of a couple to get pregnant. This inability may be due to a reproductive problem with the man, the woman, or both. Usually, a fertility problem is not diagnosed until after the couple has tried to achieve pregnancy for at least six months.

Infertility can occur for all kinds of reasons, but sometimes it's due to a hormone problem. If a man is infertile, then it may be because his testes are not producing sufficient testosterone, which is required for sperm production. Insufficient testosterone, in turn, may be due to low LH or FSH levels. LH and FSH are hormones produced by the pituitary gland. These two hormones signal the testes to produce testosterone.

An infertile woman may also have inadequate LH and FSH levels. A problem with LH or FSH may result in an inability to ovulate, or produce the eggs required for fertilization to occur. The cause of a hormone-based infertility problem may be difficult to identify. It could be due to pituitary problems, such as a tumor on the pituitary gland. It could be due to a problem with hypothalamus, such as a lesion, or injury, in the hypothalamic region of the brain. If the thyroid is not functioning correctly, then it, too, can throw hormones out of balance and possibly make it difficult to get pregnant. A woman may have polycystic ovary syndrome (PCOS) or some other medical condition that causes her to be infertile.

The only way to know for sure if hormones are the reason for infertility is through blood testing. If a blood test shows low levels of testosterone, LH, or FSH in either the man or the woman, then treatment can focus on bringing those hormones back to normal levels. Hormone therapy may include injections of any of these hormones.

The idea is that over time, the hormones in the body will reach levels sufficient for sperm production or ovulation to occur.

The drugs used to treat infertility are called gonadotropins. They include human menopausal gonadotropin (hMG) and recombinant human follicle stimulating hormone (rFSH). Human menopausal gonadotropin

Couples that have long-term trouble conceiving a baby sometimes go to a fertility clinic for help. Fertility specialists can offer a variety of medical treatments for different conditions.

contains natural FSH and LH derived from the urine of postmenopausal women, who produce lots of those two hormones. In contrast, rFSH is produced in a laboratory. A woman with low hormone levels who is not ovulating normally may take injections of either drug early in her menstrual cycle to help her develop follicles. The injections are typically given for an average of twelve days. The woman then takes human chorionic gonadotropin (hCG) to encourage ovulation. Treatment for an infertile man may also include the prescription of gonadotropins intended to bring testosterone levels in the blood into normal range.

Rarely, a pituitary tumor or hypothalamic problem is to blame for insufficient hormone levels. In these cases, surgery may be necessary. Surgical removal of a pituitary tumor, for example, followed by sufficient healing time, may be all it takes to help the gland do its job.

Hyperthyroidism and Hypothyroidism

The thyroid is little more than a bump in the throat, but it is among the most important parts of the human body. It is the anatomical equivalent of a factory, churning out hormones critical to everything from metabolism to bone growth to reproduction.

Thyroid disorders can be serious. Hyperthyroidism, a condition that results from an overactive thyroid, can lead to severe weight loss, weakness, and even heart failure. Hypothyroidism, caused by an underactive thyroid, can lead to dangerously low blood pressure, sterility, and depression, among other conditions. Thyroid cancer, another potentially dangerous condition, strikes up to twenty thousand people each year in the United States alone.

Breast Cancer

Medical experts are unsure why some people are more prone to developing breast cancer than others. However, they all agree that genetics and hormones play roles. In the case of hormones, the female hormone estrogen is especially important. Breast cancer that occurs because of hormones is termed "hormone-dependent." That is, estrogen stimulates the cancer's growth. If there are receptors for estrogen on breast cancer cells, then natural estrogen in the body can "turn on" the growth of these cells and cause the cancer to spread.

Most women know to examine their breasts regularly to monitor for any signs of a lump that may indicate the presence of breast cancer. Other signs and symptoms of breast cancer include pain and soreness, redness, and discharge or bleeding from the nipples.

A doctor screening for breast cancer will conduct a physical exam and a mammogram (breast X-ray) and may also order an ultrasound. If anything in these tests looks suspicious, then the doctor will often order a biopsy, which involves taking a sample of breast tissue for laboratory analysis.

Breast cancer is typically treated through a combination of surgery to remove the cancerous tissue (and maybe the entire breast), radiation therapy, and chemotherapy. If tests show that hormone receptors are present on the cancerous tissue, then hormone therapy will be considered as part of the treatment.

The idea behind hormone therapy for hormone-dependent breast cancer is to deprive the cancer cells of estrogen, which causes the cancer to grow and spread. The treatment tries to either reduce the amount of estrogen in the blood or prevent the estrogen receptors from working. There are several types of drugs that may work. Aromatase inhibitors lower estrogen production. Selective estrogen-receptor modulators such as tamoxifen block estrogen receptors. Estrogen-receptor down-regulators destroy estrogen receptors. Therapy may also include drugs or surgery to stop the ovaries from producing estrogen.

GYNECOMASTIA

Gynecomastia is the medical term used to describe female-like breast development in males. Caused by normal hormonal changes during puberty, the condition is relatively common and typically not dangerous. In most cases, gynecomastia goes away on its own within a few years. The hormones behind gynecomastia are estrogen and testosterone—specifically, too much estrogen compared to the amount of testosterone.

The primary medical risk with gynecomastia is the development of breast cancer. If a medical exam reveals the presence of a tumor in the breast tissue, then surgery and a combination of chemotherapy and/or radiation therapy may be required.

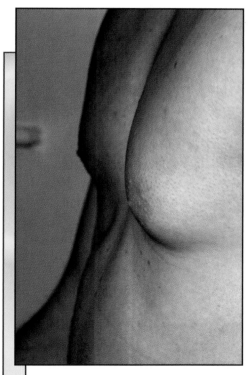

Gynecomastia is a common condition among boys going through puberty. However, this young man has female-like breast growth due to anabolic steroid abuse.

More often, the main problem with gynecomastia in teens is the mental and emotional pain associated with developing female breasts at a time when most boys are going through normal puberty. Being labeled as a social misfit—and being subjected to teasing as a result—can lead to isolation and depression.

A doctor can diagnose gynecomastia through a physical exam, taking a thorough medical history, and by conducting blood tests to measure hormone levels. Typically, diagnosis is required only to rule out other disorders or possible complications (breast cancer, for example). In most cases, no treatment is required, and the condition disappears over time as hormone levels return to normal.

CHAPTER THREE

Diagnosis and Treatment

M ost problems associated with endocrine dysfunction can be managed effectively through the use
of medications and changes in diet and lifestyle.
It's not always so easy, however. Endocrine conditions
may require a combination of therapies. Treatment may
focus on the root of the endocrine problem, on the symptoms alone, or on both. Sometimes, surgery is required to
help fix an endocrine problem. Some people turn to alternative treatments, seeking help through acupuncture,
massage, aromatherapy, or other methods.

DIAGNOSIS

Diagnosing an endocrine problem begins with a visit to a
doctor. That may be a family physician, a pediatrician, or
an endocrinologist. Pediatric endocrinologists are
endocrinologists who specialize in helping children with
endocrine conditions.

The doctor will conduct a thorough medical history,
asking the patient for relevant details about his or her

past—anything from information on recent illnesses to surgical procedures. After taking a medical history, the physician will do a physical exam, looking for any outward signs of illness. The height and weight of the patient will be measured, as will blood pressure and pulse. It's important to get an idea of the patient's general overall health. Next, the doctor might request blood tests to check hormone levels, and he or she might order genetic testing to see if an inherited condition is behind the symptoms. Finally, the doctor might order imaging tests to take a look inside the body. These tests could include ultrasound, CT scans, and/or MRIs.

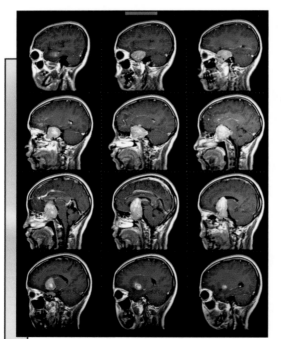

MRI is an imaging technique used to provide an internal view of organs. This MRI reveals a tumor in the pituitary gland.

TREATMENT

The broad range of endocrine disorders requires a broad range of treatment options. Common therapies involve medications or surgery, and, often, a combination of the two.

For some patients with endocrine system issues, surgery may be required to help them function normally and/or look more normal. "Feminizing genital surgery," for instance, may be appropriate for female infants who have external male genitalia because of congenital adrenal hyperplasia (CAH). On the other hand, a baby boy with female sexual characteristics my require "masculinizing genital surgery." Feminizing and masculinizing procedures often require other corrective surgeries later in life, especially during puberty. Many patients also require additional hormone therapy.

If test results lead the doctor to diagnose an endocrine disorder, then medications may be administered. Of course, the medications will depend on the condition, but they may include drugs to stimulate or reduce the production of certain hormones. After a period, the doctor will order follow-up tests to see whether the medications are working as intended.

Drug therapy may not be effective if the cause of an endocrine condition is a tumor in the hypothalamus or pituitary gland. In such cases, surgery may be required to remove the tumor. The operation is typically performed by a neurosurgeon, a doctor who specializes in brain and spine surgery. The size of the tumor and its location will determine how the doctor accesses and removes it. In many cases, endoscopic surgery can remove the tumor safely. This is a minimally invasive type of procedure involving the use of a very thin tube called an endoscope, which is inserted through the nose. The key aspect of endoscopy is video technology. A camera mounted on the tip of the

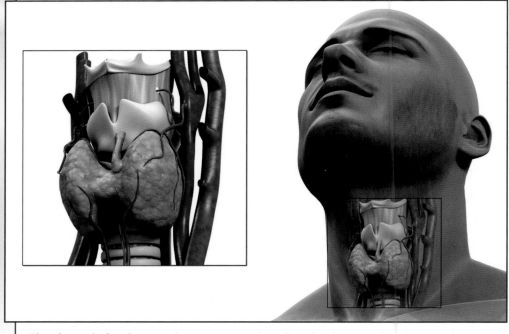

The thyroid gland, an endocrine organ found in the front of the throat, releases thyroid hormone. Thyroid hormone plays a critical role in growth and metabolism.

endoscope magnifies the surgical area by about twenty times, enabling surgeons to clearly see what they're doing.

THYROID SURGERY

Endoscopic surgery may also be used to remove a diseased thyroid. When the thyroid is removed, the patient begins a lifetime of thyroid hormone therapy (medically prescribed thyroid hormone pills), and life goes on almost as normal.

Thyroid surgery is commonplace and removal of this organ is rarely complicated, but there are drawbacks.

There's the scar, for one. Conventional thyroid surgery leaves a several-inch-long gash across the front of the lower neck, and for many patients this scar can linger for years. Recovery time, too, can be longer than one might expect. Patients often must stay in the hospital for a couple of days before they are sent home.

Fortunately, thanks to advances in surgical techniques, more patients are going home sooner after the surgery. Now, surgeons can remove the thyroid with a much smaller incision, a lot less blood loss, and in a way that allows patients to go home in a matter of hours. The same techniques are increasingly being used in other surgical procedures as well.

One technique, the minimally invasive thyroidectomy, involves surgeons working through a small, 1.5-inch (3.8-centimeter) incision. Another technique, endoscopy, requires an even smaller incision and uses an ultrasonic harmonic scalpel. The scalpel blade vibrates back and forth thousands of times every second, using frictional energy to make the incision. The energy from the scalpel seals blood vessels to limit the amount of bleeding, even as the cutting proceeds. The result: much cleaner, smaller incisions requiring no external stitches.

The standard approach to thyroid surgery and other surgeries will always be necessary for some. However, as surgeons adopt more advanced techniques, many patients will experience easier recoveries and, most important, return home faster to continue on with their lives.

CHAPTER FOUR

Prevention

Not all endocrine conditions are preventable. Genetics plays a large role in some of the more common disorders, and your genetic makeup is beyond your control. In addition, endocrine issues can be caused by tumors or injuries, which usually have more to do with bad luck than poor prevention. Nevertheless, there are things one can do to reduce the risk of complications from an endocrine disease. Maintaining good general health is most important. It is the key to keeping the body strong and preventing endocrine conditions from occurring in the first place.

SYSTEM MAINTENANCE AND CARE

It's up for debate how much the environment influences human endocrine biology. However, there are things one can do to maintain good general health and (hopefully) ward off problems before they become serious. Doctors and other medical professionals around the world recommend a healthy diet full of nutritious fruits and vegetables, whole grains, and unprocessed foods. By eating well, it's easier to maintain a healthy weight and a healthy heart. If the body is functioning well, then the endocrine system benefits, too.

To maintain optimal endocrine system health, some people recommend avoiding exposure to synthetic (human-produced) chemicals. In particular, this means avoiding foods produced using chemical pesticides or herbicides. Others think the danger of synthetic chemicals is exaggerated. If you're concerned, then you can try to eat organic food products, which are grown and produced using only natural substances.

A healthy lifestyle naturally results in better functioning body systems. Regular exercise is one of the keys to staying healthy.

The general recommendations for healthy living apply to anyone seeking better endocrine health. That is, increase your exercising to at least half an hour three days a week, and more (much more) if possible. Don't smoke. Smoking compromises the immune system, making it more likely that you will get sick. It also leads to deadly diseases such as cancer. Eat well, stay fit, and see a doctor for regular checkups. By visiting a doctor once or twice a year, you increase the odds of diagnosing a disease before it becomes serious. Doctors know what to look for. Through general physical exams, evaluations, and blood tests, they can get a good snapshot of how your body is doing and they will make recommendations if anything needs to change.

PLAYING IT SAFE

This book discusses the endocrine system and the way it affects sexual health. Any serious discussion of sexual health must include talk about safe sex. If you are not sexually active, then that's great—you have much less to worry about when it comes to your sexual health. Those who do have sex, at any age, should always use a condom. In addition to preventing unwanted pregnancies, condoms provide protection against sexually transmitted diseases (STDs). Such diseases, including HIV/AIDS, chlamydia, gonorrhea, herpes, and syphilis, can lead to serious health issues. STDs might not directly harm the endocrine system, but they lead to a decline in overall health, which makes the endocrine system more vulnerable.

Anabolic steroid use is another serious issue when it comes to endocrine health. Those who take steroids increase their risk for developing endocrine problems. The body processes artificial steroids just as it does the natural ones it's already producing. Using human growth hormone, or HGH, is equally dangerous. By taking "performance-enhancing" drugs, people risk throwing their endocrine system completely out of whack. Hormone levels in the bloodstream may rise to dangerous levels, for example, and lead to all kinds of health issues—everything from gynecomastia and infertility in men to amenorrhea and the growth of facial hair in women. Thrown off by the artificial hormones, the body may lose its ability to regulate natural hormone levels.

Ultimately, maintaining good sexual health—and good overall health—is about making good decisions throughout one's life. It's important to set goals and to take steps to achieve those goals while always keeping your health in mind.

Ten Great Questions to Ask Your Endocrinologist

1. What are my treatment options?

2. Are there any side effects or risks associated with these treatments?

3. What are the benefits of each treatment?

4. Will I need to return for follow-up exams?

5. Are there alternative approaches to treatment that might be effective—things such as acupuncture, chiropracty, or counseling?

6. What can I do to improve my overall health?

7. Are there any support groups in the area that I can join for help?

8. Will I miss any school because of treatment?

9. Can I continue playing sports and taking part in other school and after-school activities?

10. What, if anything, does my condition mean for me in the future, when I'm an adult?

CHAPTER FIVE

Coping and Support

I t can be tremendously difficult to cope with an endocrine disorder. Depending on the particular symptoms of the disorder, an individual might have to live with anything from infertility to unwanted hair or genitals. These are physical challenges. There are emotional challenges, too, to coping with endocrine diseases.

Managing an intersex disorder, for example, is extremely difficult emotionally. An intersex disorder (like some CAH cases, discussed in chapter 2) is a condition in which a male develops female genitalia or a female develops male genitalia. Sometimes, intersex disorders occur when sex hormones adversely affect the development of the growing fetus. For instance, prenatal androgen exposure can cause a baby girl to develop external genitals similar to those of a boy. A male fetus, on the other hand, may lack the ability to respond to the androgens in his bloodstream. In that case, he might be born with a clitoris and other structures suggestive of female anatomy.

Surgery may be performed on a baby to correct an intersex disorder. For example, unwanted sex glands can be removed in a procedure called gonadectomy. Along with hormone therapy, gonadectomy usually resolves the major physical abnormalities of an intersex disorder. Future problems can arise, however, if a boy or girl identifies more with the opposite gender than with the one he or she has been assigned. When they grow up, these individuals who have had corrective surgery may ultimately decide to seek "gender reassignment." That is,

Cheryl Chase *(above)* is the founder of the Intersex Society of North America. Her group works to educate the public about children born with both male and female sex characteristics.

they may once again undergo corrective surgery, this time to restore their anatomy to the sex they feel they were born to be.

Individuals with gender identity issues face enormous psychological challenges, especially if they don't have the support of family, friends, and others in their community. They may feel isolated and avoid intimate relationships for fear of being rejected. In addition, they may struggle with a host of other social and physical issues. (Infertility, for example, is one common side effect.)

The most important thing a person with an intersex disorder or any other endocrine disorder can do is to seek help. It doesn't matter whether that's through a doctor, counseling, the support of friends and family, or through local and regional support groups. Some may wish to receive all the help they can get. Others might only look to a trusted endocrinologist who they know will maintain their privacy while providing the treatment they need.

In all cases, communication is the key to successful treatment. In addition to their intended effects, hormone medications can have side effects, including mood swings, depression, and hair development or hair loss. It's important that the patient tells his or her endocrinologist what the effects are so that dosages may be adjusted accordingly.

Endocrine disorders can be hard to deal with. It's not unusual to feel embarrassed around classmates or friends, especially if there are noticeable symptoms of the disorder for everyone to see. However, keeping things bottled up inside will only make the condition even more difficult to bear. This is why it's so important for an individual to open up and talk about his or her feelings.

SUPPORT GROUPS AND HOTLINES

When you're looking for help and you feel like no one around you understands what you're going through, a hotline can be a great source of information. Hotlines are usually toll-free telephone numbers that you can call to talk to someone who is knowledgeable about the disease or condition in question. The people who answer your call can point you in the right direction if you'd like more information or assistance. Two well-known hotlines for general medical information include the National Women's Health Information Center (NWHIC) at (800) 994-9662 and the National Institute of Child Health and Human Development at (800) 370-2943.

Support groups are another potentially useful resource. Support groups are small gatherings of people sharing similar challenges. Sometimes, just hearing someone else's story can make your own situation feel more bearable. Support groups are great places to go to find compassionate friends when it seems like no one else understands.

There are online support groups; local groups that meet in town halls, churches, or schools; and groups that meet over the phone through "teleconference." A good way to find a local support group is by asking at a local health clinic, by checking the phone book, or by looking for events listed at local community resource centers, such as a YMCA or church. Online groups often maintain Web sites and listservs that members can use to interact with each other.

Helping Others

If you don't have an endocrine problem but know someone who does, then you may be wondering what you can do

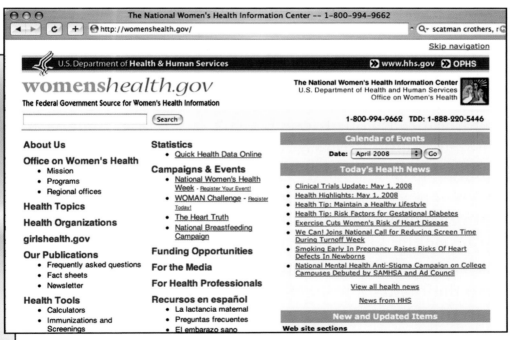

You can visit the Web site of the National Women's Health Information Center (www.womenshealth.gov) to learn more about endocrine system disorders and other issues related to women's health.

to help. It's natural to want to help. After all, if it were you, then you'd appreciate it if other people offered their care and support.

You can help a friend or family member just by being available to listen. Talk to the person about his or her feelings, and listen to what he or she has to say. You can also help by being a resource for more information. Tell your friend if you know of any local support groups or if you know someone else with the same condition. Any help you can offer will be appreciated. Even if it turns out that you can't help, or your friend doesn't want your help, it never hurts to try.

If a friend is in a situation where he or she has to miss school for treatment, then you can help by talking to teachers, collecting assignments, and taking notes. It's important that your friend doesn't fall behind in class. You can help out by acting as your friend's eyes and ears while he or she is away.

Whenever you offer to help someone, keep in mind that privacy and confidentiality are top priorities. It may not be public knowledge that the person has a certain disease or condition. People who are sick may want to keep their situation secret—or at least limited to a few close friends.

Ten Facts About the Endocrine System

1. Most women experience menopause around the age of fifty.

2. There is a slightly increased risk of breast cancer among premenopausal women who have received combination hormone therapy (taking both estrogen and progestin) for more than five years. Among the same group, there is a reduced risk of ovarian cancer.

3. Use of illegal anabolic steroids by young adults can lead to stunted growth, irritability, depression, and other highly dangerous side effects.

4. Up to thirty million U.S. men experience erectile dysfunction, or trouble achieving or maintaining an erection. Only a small percentage of these men have hormone problems.

5. Many chemicals commonly used in conventional (nonorganic) agriculture are known endocrine disruptors. When absorbed by the body in unhealthy amounts, they can disrupt normal functions by blocking hormone circulation, altering hormone levels, and preventing hormone production.

6. The human endocrine system affects every cell in the body.

7. Hormonal problems often go undiagnosed because signs and symptoms may be either lacking or similar to those of many different diseases and conditions.

8. About 75 percent of menstruating women experience some form of premenstrual syndrome, or PMS. Only a small percentage, however, experience a more severe kind of PMS called premenstrual dysphoric disorder (PMDD).

9. Synthetic chemicals in the environment, including dioxins and PCBs, can interfere with the endocrine system's ability to function.

10. Gynecomastia, or the development of female-like breasts in males, usually goes away in time without treatment.

GLOSSARY

adrenal glands Endocrine glands that release aldosterone, cortisol, testosterone, epinephrine, and norepinephrine.

disorder Disease or medical problem.

endocrine gland Gland that produces hormone and then secretes it directly into the blood.

endocrine system Body system responsible for hormone secretion.

endocrinologist One who studies the endocrine system and is an expert on endocrine diseases and treatment.

endocrinology Study of the endocrine system.

estrogen Female sex hormone produced primarily by the ovaries.

gland Organ that produces and secretes substances.

gonads Main reproductive organs, including the testes (male) and the ovaries (female).

hormone Molecule released by endocrine glands into the blood and which serves as a chemical messenger between cells.

hypothalamus Endocrine organ located in the brain; regulates other endocrine glands.

infertile Unable to have children.

menopause Period of life when a woman's menstrual cycle ceases, usually beginning around the age of fifty.

menstruation Period; the phase of the menstrual cycle when bleeding occurs as the uterine lining is shed.

organ Body part with a specialized function.

ovaries Female reproductive organs where eggs are produced.

parathyroid glands Endocrine glands on the back of the thyroid that secrete parathyroid hormone.

pituitary gland Major endocrine gland located below the hypothalamus in the brain.

placenta Organ that nourishes the developing fetus during pregnancy.

polycystic ovary syndrome (PCOS) Condition characterized by multiple cysts, or small, sac-like growths, on the ovaries.

premenstrual Occurring just before menstruation.

receptor Specific molecule on or in a cell that recognizes and binds with other specific molecules, including hormones.

testosterone Male sex hormone produced primarily by the testes.

thymus Endocrine gland that releases hormones important for the immune system.

thyroid gland Endocrine gland that releases thyroid hormone.

FOR MORE INFORMATION

Health Canada
Address Locator 0900C2
Ottawa, ON K1A 0K9
Canada
(866) 225-0709
Web site: http://www.hc-sc.gc.ca
Health Canada is Canada's federal agency responsible for
    helping citizens maintain and improve their health.

The Hormone Foundation
8401 Connecticut Avenue, Suite 900
Chevy Chase, MD 20815
(800) HOR-MONE (467-6663)
Web site: http://www.hormone.org
This foundation is a leading source of information on the
    endocrine system and related diseases.

National Institutes of Health (NIH)
9000 Rockville Pike
Bethesda, MD 20892
(301) 496-4000
Web site: http://www.nih.gov

Part of the U.S. Department of Health and Human
  Services, the NIH is the primary federal agency for
  conducting and supporting medical research, including
  studies on children's and teen's health.

U.S. Centers for Disease Control and Prevention (CDC)
1600 Clifton Road
Atlanta, GA 30333
(800) CDC-INFO (232-4636)
Web site: http://www.cdc.gov
The CDC is a large public health agency whose goal is to
  promote health and quality of life by preventing and
  controlling disease, injury, and disability.

WEB SITES

Due to the changing nature of Internet links, Rosen
Publishing has developed an online list of Web sites
related to the subject of this book. This site is updated
regularly. Please use this link to access the list:

http://www.rosenlinks.com/lsh/ensy

FOR FURTHER READING

Kim, Melissa, and Susan Dudley Gold. *The Endocrine and Reproductive Systems*. Berkeley Heights, NJ: Enslow Publishers, 2003.

Little, Marjorie. *The Endocrine System*. New York, NY: Chelsea House, 2000.

Olien, Rebecca. *The Endocrine System*. Mankato, MN: Bridgestone Books/Capstone Press, 2006.

Rushton, Lynette. *The Endocrine System*. New York, NY: Chelsea House, 2004.

Watson, Stephanie, and Kelli Miller. *The Endocrine System*. Westport, CT: Greenwood Press, 2004.

Wood, Elaine, and Pamela Walker. *Understanding the Human Body—The Endocrine System*. Farmington Hills, MI: Lucent Books, 2003.

BIBLIOGRAPHY

American Cancer Society. "Detailed Guide: Pituitary Tumor Surgery." November 9, 2006. Retrieved February 8, 2008 (http://www.cancer.org/docroot/CRI/content/CRI_2_4_4X_Surgery_61.asp?rnav=cri).

BreastCancer.org. "What Role Do Hormones Play in Breast Cancer Treatment?" July 26, 2007. Retrieved February 8, 2008 (http://www.breastcancer.org/treatment/hormonal/what_is_it/hormone_role.jsp).

Campbell, Neil, Jane Reece, and Lawrence Mitchell. *Biology*. 5th ed. Menlo Park, CA: Benjamin/Cummings, 1999.

Colorado State University. "Pathophysiology of the Endocrine System." April 30, 2006. Retrieved February 7, 2008 (http://www.vivo.colostate.edu/hbooks/pathphys/endocrine).

Ganong, William F. *Review of Medical Physiology*. 19th ed. Stamford, CT: Appleton & Lange, 1999.

Healthwise, Inc. "Gonadotropin Treatment for Infertility." WebMD, April 7, 2006. Retrieved February 18, 2008 (http://www.webmd.com/infertility-and-reproduction/gonadotropin-treatment-for-infertility#hw201767).

The Hormone Foundation. "Diseases & Conditions." 2008. Retrieved February 9, 2008 (http://www.hormone.org/public/conditions.cfm).

Houk, Christopher P., et al. "Summary of Consensus Statement on Intersex Disorders and Their Management." *Pediatrics*, August 1, 2006. Retrieved February 3, 2008 (http://www.pediatrics. aappublications.org/cgi/content/full/118/2/753).

Intersex Society of North America. "Frequently Asked Questions." 1993–2006. Retrieved May 15, 2008 (http://www.isna.org/faq).

Netdoctor. "Oestrogel." July 24, 2006. Retrieved May 12, 2008 (www.netdoctor.co.uk/medicines/100001917.html).

The Patient Education Institute. "X-Plain Low Testosterone Reference Summary." 2005. Retrieved February 14, 2008 (http://www.nlm.nih.gov/medlineplus/tutorials/ lowtestosterone/ur189101.pdf).

Snow, Ayelet, et al. "Severe Hypersomnolence After Pituitary/Hypothalamic Surgery in Adolescents: Clinical Characteristics and Potential Mechanisms." *Pediatrics*, December 2002. Retrieved February 8, 2008 (http://pediatrics.aappublications.org/cgi/ content/full/110/6/e74).

U.S. Department of Health and Human Services. "Polycystic Ovary Syndrome (PCOS)." WomensHealth.gov, April 2007. Retrieved February 14, 2008 (http://www. forwomen.gov/faq/pcos.htm).

U.S. Food and Drug Administration. "Bio-Identicals: Sorting Myths from Facts." January 9, 2008. Retrieved February 14, 2008 (http://www.fda.gov/consumer/ updates/bioidenticals010908.html).

BIBLIOGRAPHY

Welt, Corrine K. "Patient Information: Menstrual Cycle
  Disorders (Absent and Irregular Periods)."
  UpToDate.com. August 21, 2006. Retrieved February
  17, 2008 (http://www.patients.uptodate.com/topic.
  asp?file = endocrin/9299&title = Menstrual + cycle).

INDEX

ABOUT THE AUTHOR

Michael R. Wilson is a health and science writer. He has written about many topics for Rosen Publishing, including the human brain, the cardiopulmonary system, and genetics.

PHOTO CREDITS

Cover © www.istockphoto.com/Chris Schmidt; p. 1 © www.istockphoto.com/Luis Carlos Torres; p. 4 © www.istockphoto.com/ericsphotography; p. 4 (silhouette) © www.istockphoto.com/jamesbenet; p. 7 Stephen Mallon/Photonica/Getty Images; p. 9 © pttmedical/Newscom; p. 18 © GARO/PHANIE/Photo Researchers, Inc.; p. 21 © Shaun Botterill/Getty Images; p. 23 © krtweeklyfeaturelive/Newscom; p. 27 Marwan Naamani/AFP/Getty Images; p. 31 Per-Anders Pettersson/Getty Images; p. 35 © Dr. P. Marazzi/Photo Researchers, Inc.; p. 38 © www.istockphoto.com/Dean Hoch; p. 40 MedicalRF.com/Getty Images; p. 43 © www.istockphoto.com/Michael Krinke; p. 48 © AP Images; Back cover (top to bottom) 3D4Medical.com/Getty Images, © www.istockphoto.com/Luis Carlos Torres, © www.istockphoto.com/Kiyoshi Takahase Segundo, CDC, © www.istockphoto.com/Amanda Rohde, Scott Bodell/Photodisc/Getty Images.

Designer: Nelson Sá; **Editor:** Christopher Roberts
Photo Researcher: Amy Feinberg